ANOTHER
SHORT &
SWEET
BOOK BY

Becky Brown

www.ShortandSweetBooks.com

Also by Rebecca Brown:

How to Make As in eCollege

The definitive guide to finding
the right online school, making top grades
and finally getting the job you deserve.
www.ShortandSweetBooks.com

HOW TO TEACH ONLINE

And Make $100,000 A Year!

Develop an Income Stream,
Diversify Your Teaching Portfolio
Learn the Joy of Working
When and Where You Choose

Rebecca Brown, M.A.

Contents

A Word from the Author

About four and a half years ago I saw an ad on the web that said if I had a Master's degree I could teach college online and make extra money in my spare time. It sounded crazy and I was very suspicious, but I answered the ad anyway.

Almost immediately, I was contacted by a faculty recruiter for the University of Phoenix. Thus began a three-month application process that included rounding up official copies of all my transcripts, getting together a CV that emphasized my teaching experience (not much of that in the beginning), and taking training courses online at UOP.

Finally, I had my first class and my first roster of students. I wrote my own lectures and discussion questions. I seemed to be online day and night cruising the newsgroups looking for students to talk to, and I found the whole experience exhausting and exhilarating.

Since then, I have been building my vita with experience teaching many different humanities and composition classes at many different schools.

It was sometime during the second year that it occurred to me that I could make more than just a little spare change at this kind of work.

Traditionally, adjuncts have been graduates just out of their MA or PhD programs trying to pay the bills while they found a fulltime teaching job. Colleges and universities traditionally hired adjuncts to pick up the extra classes that needed to be filled after all the fulltime faculty had their full loads for the semester.

So an adjunct could get a class at the local community college to teach, and another one or two across town at the state University. No single class paid very much and adjuncts were notoriously poor. Because all classes were taught in physical buildings, adjuncts were restrained by the physical distance they could drive each day to reach their classes. No adjunct could manage more than about four classes, even if they were offered more.

Well, the model has changed!

Now, according to *Adjunct Nation*, nearly 40-50% of all college classes are taught by adjuncts rather than fulltime faculty. And with the advent of the online universities there is a whole new market for parttime faculty.

But the really significant difference for fulltime adjuncts is that now they, just like their students, can work from a home office. Without the restraints of the physical classroom and calculating travel time, an adjunct can finally accept enough classes to earn a respectable living. They can handle 5, 7, 9 classes at a time.

Additionally, because online universities generally discard the semester convention and schedule many sections of the same class, each starting just a week or two apart, there are plenty of classes to teach.

It is this new economy of distance education that has suddenly open the doors to higher education for millions of students who were denied it before. It has also offered new employment for thousands of educators who now have the opportunity to earn an income that is worthy of the job they perform.

In this manual for success as a fulltime online adjunct, I try to be as candid in my discussion of how this industry works, and in my evaluations of the schools I have personal experience with, as I possibly can. If I think a school is abusive of its facultys' time, I will tell you. If I think they put

profit-earning (and the majority of these schools

are for-profit institutions, unlike their brick & mor-

tar sisters) I will tell you. This is a new and quickly

growing industry. It is our responsibility—the facul-

ty who work in it—to monitor and shape the way

it grows.

I welcome your own evaluations and ex-

periences. Please correct me if you find that my

data is mistaken our out-dated. I would love to

hear about your personal experiences on the

TeacherTalk forum on our website (www.How-

ToTeachOnline.com).

But most of all, I wish you the best fortune

in your use of this manual. I know the process of

applying to and building your teaching schedule

can seem daunting at first. But before you know

it, your monthly income will begin to feel more

and more robust, and the security you will know

when you control where you teach and how

much you teach will put you above and beyond

those more traditionally employed friends of

yours!

-Becky Brown

Teaching Requirements

Every online school has different requirements for their instructors, from professional degrees and licenses to plain old Bachelor of Arts and practical working experience. So you need to find out exactly what each school looks for, and make sure you fit those requirements before you apply. We'll talk more about this in the section on writing your Curriculum Vita.

Educational Requirements

Most schools that are accredited will require an advanced degree from their faculty. That means more than a B.A., such as an M.A., M.F.A., Ph.D. or J.D. They also likely want you to be experienced in your field. So if you plan to teach law, and you just graduated from law school, you're outta luck. You will have to have at least two years of solid legal experience before you can start teaching using that degree.

If you do have a terminal degree, however, or at least an M.A. and plenty of experience, then you should have no trouble getting teaching assignments.

Transcripts

Many schools will require that you have official or unofficial transcripts sent to them along with your application. If you have grade reports from your last semester of graduate school, and that shows your grades in every class, that will suffice as unofficial transcripts. You can make a copy and send that in with your application.

For official transcripts you will have to contact your graduate program and have those sent directly to the school where you're applying for a job. Official transcripts come with an official seal – so it's no good sending them to yourself to forward on. They have to go directly to the recruiters at the school where you're applying.

Most universities and colleges these days have websites where you can order your transcripts online. There is a nominal fee (about $5) for each transcript you send. And each school you apply to will need their own official transcripts.

I know, I know, seems like a lot of wasted energy and money, but keep your eye on the ball —once you've been accepted as a teacher, you'll be raking in the money. This is just your initial investment.

Recommendations
You will probably also need several recommendations from business associates or colleagues. Just like in any job, choose people who like you and can write well (don't choose that boss that fired you for being late to work or the one that can't put together two words without misspelling one).

It helps to keep recommendations on file so

that you can send them out each time you ap-
~~ply for a teaching position. And as I will explain~~
later, you want to apply to a lot of colleges!

So ask your associates to write a good, generic
recommendation (i.e., not addressed to any
particular person or school) and include that
in your application packet when requested.

Remember, the last part of applying for a job is
sending the recommendations, so don't send
them with your query letter or your resume.
Wait until the prospective employer asks for it.

Curriculum Vita

Yup, that's your resume. In academia we call
it the Curriculum Vita or CV. (In Europe they
call all resumes CVs. Go figure.)

The difference between a business world resume
and a CV is that in the CV you put absolutely
everything you have ever done or accomplished!
Even put things you have just attempted and
didn't quite finish.

Your CV is not the best of you, like in the business world, it is all of you. So naturally it should
be several pages.

What to include in your Curriculum Vita

1. Anything you've ever written

2. Anything you've ever published

3. Any award you've ever won (even second place in that poetry contest in college)

4. Every school you've ever attended

5. Your GPA, only if it's better than 3.0

6. Every club of which you've been a member

7. Every office you've ever held, in any club

8. Any internship, assistantship, or work study you've done with a professor

9. Any time you've ever taught a class (even when you filled in for one of your profs and all you did was hand out papers and grade quizzes).

10. Any work you've done that could possibly relate to the classes you want to teach. (Were you the secretary at an ad agency? Wasn't that a lot of writing, editing, and communications? Put it down.)

11. Any job you've ever held that required you to write, think, teach, communicate or invent.

12. Any traveling you did for work. (Okay, I don't think you can parlay that snorkling vacation to Tobago into work experience, but who knows! Maybe you're a better writer than me.)

13. What else is there? It's your life, brainstorm a little bit. Be honest, but be fair to yourself, too!

Customize your CV for each job (do I really have to say this?). You need to make sure that if you are applying to teach math, that your CV emphasizes all the math experience you've had. If applying to teach English, emphasis on writing and communications. Don't even think you can write one CV and use it for everything!

Customize your cover letter too. (Huh, never would have thought that!) The cover letter is where you "talk" to the online recruiter. So make it friendly and personal.

Remember, one of the things you want to show is that you can reflect an energetic, friendly personality merely through the words you write. How you write is how your students will "see" you. And that's what the faculty recruiters will be thinking about when they read your cover letter and CV. So your email is your first introduction – it is how you will interest prospective employers in hiring you as an instructor for their students. Make it friendly, open, personable.

All right, now you have your CV done and your cover letter written, and you've sent it in and been contacted by a faculty recruiter. Hooray! That was easy. Yep, this is a growing business, so there are lots of positions out there for qualified instructors. But now you have to fill out their application.

Generally this includes a very long, complicated packet of materials, including affidavits, photos, transcripts, etc. Often much of this can be done online. But some schools will still snail-mail this packet to you. Don't wait, fill it out right away and send it in fast. Most schools have rotating and overlapping course schedules, so there are classes starting every week. The faster you send in your application, the faster you will get approved and be assigned a class – and the sooner you will start feeling that new income stream.

The most important part of the application is your personal statement. This is the place where you show the prospective school that you fit their ideal of online faculty. So spend some time on this. Polish and perfect. Have someone proofread. (How can you ask to teach English composition if your application is full of typos and spelling errors?)

What they really want to hear in this statement is why you will make an excellent online instructor. They want to hear that you love teaching, that you love teaching adult students and are aware of the different methods involved in teaching adult students. They want to hear your "tone" (there's that important word again) and know that you can communicate online with warmth and encouragement. Your statement is where you show them all this.

Time Commitment

Okay, so now you've got a good idea of what you need to do in order to get your foot in the door and start teaching classes. But what you really want to know is how much time this is going to take.

Obviously, it will take a little while to build up your teaching schedule so you are earning six figures (I teach 10 or more classes at a time in order to earn that amount) and maybe you don't need that much money. Maybe you have a day job that you love and don't plan to give it up. Maybe this is just a supplement to your regular income. Or maybe, you have other artistic goals. (Any painters, writers, actors out there?) This is the income stream that will enable you to pursue that goal. So how much time will you have to spend teaching, grading and taking seminars in order to earn this money?

The easy answer is, just as much time as you choose. You are a subcontractor, and each class is a new contract that you can choose to accept or decline depending on your schedule. Want to spend the summer in Greece, don't accept any classes during the summer. Need to earn a little extra dough for Christmas, accept a lot of classes during the fall.

I can't tell you how much time it will take you to facilitate each class you teach at each school. They vary so much. But I can tell you how to maximize your proficiency and increase the number of classes you can efficiently handle at once. For more about that, see Chapter 4: Optimizing Your Teaching.

The rule of thumb is that each class takes approximately 10-20 hours per week to facilitate. Well, that is how the schools calculate it. Okay, you're doing the math and you're now asking yourself how I can work 140-280 hours a week at this. Like I said before, process is everything. I certainly don't work anywhere near 140 hours a week. (Are there 140 hours in a week?) I do work 35-40 hours per week when I am carrying a full load of classes. Which for me is 14 – 20 classes at once.

Remember, many of the schools where you teach will assign you several sections of the same class, and they often overlap. So you might have two sections of HUM102 starting on Monday, and another two starting the next Monday. So by the second week you will be teaching 4 classes of HUM102.

But the way I think about it is that I have 80 students taking HUM102, since I have about 20 students per class. Forty of those are in their first week of the class, and 40 are in their second week. Since I've already put together all my materials for each class and know exactly what to upload when, I can focus on facilitating discussions, answering questions, and grading assignments. Which takes me a lot less that 10 hours per class. (See Chapter 3 for more about organizing classes and optimizing workloads.)

To start, you will be slow. It will all seem confusing and difficult and very time consuming. You will feel like you need to be online all the time. You will have no boundaries and feel tied to your computer. Don't let that dissuade you! There is a very steep learning curve with this job. It's really hard in the beginning. But once you master the technology and develop your own methods you will suddenly find yourself with a lot of free time on your hands; time to paint, write the great American novel, walk the dog, play with the kids, cook gourmet meals, travel, snuggle with your significant other.

Adult Learners are Different . . .

No matter what you look like on paper, the biggest requirement for any online instructor is that they love teaching, and they are good at communicating online.

Hm . . . doesn't sound hard, right? Well, it's hard!

Think of it this way, your students never ever see your face. They don't hear your voice (for the most part) and can't hear that wry tone you use when you crack jokes or the smile you use when you say something a bit sarcastic.

They only "hear" what they see. Tone is extremely important, and I discuss this in detail in Chapter 4: Avoiding Problems – maybe the most important chapter in this manual!

Remember, you're teaching adult learners who either never had the opportunity to go to school in the first place, or who went and failed in some important way.

These students are your contemporaries, and they are also wary of college and anything like professors. Some think they can't do the work, many believe this will just be another way for them to fail.

Most hope like heck that this time they will find out they are bright, responsible and capable students and that this experience will be the start of a new, better life. Your job is to convince them that they are and it will.

So if you are not the cheerleader type, or if you think discipline is the best way to drive a point home, this is probably not the job for you.

Selecting Schools

ow that you have an overview of all that is entailed in teaching online, you need to pick your schools. Every school has a slightly different model for teaching online classes. And as this industry proves more and more profitable, more and more schools are joining the ranks of virtual environments. That's a good thing! More work for you and me. But it also means that if you follow my plan, and diversify your employment opportunities, you will need to keep track of each school's rules and regulations for teaching.

So I suggest you start off by being selective about which schools you apply to. Many provide the class modules already developed and ready to teach. All you have to do is facilitate them. But some schools want their instructors to create the classes as well as facilitate them. And some want you to teach the students how to use the technology too. I think this is crazy!

Your goal as an instructor is to focus on the learning of your students, not to teach them how to use their computers (unless you're actually teaching IT) or to create class modules for schools—unless you get paid extra for that extra work!

Remember, you get paid a set rate per class, so the only way to make this job a reasonable method of supporting yourself is to become efficient at managing your time. You won't be efficient if you take on the jobs of developers and tech-support. You won't be able to focus on teaching if you become administration too.

As you look through the list of schools and programs in the back of this book I suggest you jot down the pay for each class, responsibilities of faculty, pay periods (for instance, do you get paid monthly based on your teaching schedules, or do you get paid a bulk amount at the end of each class you teach), holiday schedules (some schools I teach for do not include any holidays, and I have often found myself Christmas morning grading papers while unwrapping presents), 401ks, stock options, class sizes, teaching limits, etc.

Pay Scale

Most online schools pay you per class. You are a subcontractor and each time they offer you a class and you accept it, you sign a contract to complete that class—and only that class. Accepting one class does not mean you will ever be offered another. Accepting 20 classes does not mean you will ever be offered another.

But if you make yourself a valuable contractor that faculty schedulers can rely on and students love, then you will almost always continue to be offered classes.

Pay for Each Class is Not High

Part of the quandry for adjuncts is that they are paid so little for each class. That problem is magnified when classes are compressed into

4-5 weeks, as they are in most online schools.
You end up doing the same amount of work
in 5 weeks as you would in a full semester-long
course, but get paid a quarter of what on-
ground, fulltime faculty are paid. Somewhere between $1,200 - $1,500 for each completed class.

Just for comparison, the American Historical Asso-
ciation, in addressing the growing use of adjuncts
to teach the majority of college courses, recom-
mended that these parttime teachers be paid at
least 80% of what their fulltime brethren are paid:

*This would mean, for example, that if an assistant
professor teaches six courses and is paid $40,000 a
year, the per-course payment for a part-time faculty
person should be (at the 80 percent rate) $5,300 per
course; if the salary was the same and the course
load was 8 courses a year, the pay should be $4,000
per course; if 10 courses a year, the pay should
be $3,200 per course. The amount paid should be
increased over time to recognize years in service.
(AHA-OAH permanent Committee on Part-time and
Adjunct Employment, 2003)*

Obviously, this is not how our industry works today,
and until it is we need to be sure that we work for
reasonable pay and monitor the amount of time
it takes to teach each class.

Calculate Your Weekly Pay

I like to figure the pay scale per week so I can compare apples to apples when evaluating where I want to teach. A class contract that runs nine weeks and pays $1,400 comes to about $155 per week. A five week class that pays $960 per contract, comes to about $192 per week.

So if you want to earn $10,000 per month (which I do – and often earn more than that) you need to keep about 14 classes rotating through your teaching schedule; the bulk of those 14 will be the $155 a week classes, with some of the higher paying classes to help bump up your monthly income.

Calculate Your Hourly Pay

Since each school has different requirements for how much time you must spend online, and how many assignments you have to grade, it's always a good idea to calculate your hourly wage after you've finished with each class. Just so you know how much you are actually being paid for your time online.

I have discovered that some classes that seem to pay well on a weekly basis, require so much of my time that my hourly pay is quite low. Once you start teaching and have a full portfolio, you can begin refining it by looking at what you earn for each school hourly and drop those schools (or at least limit them to one class a year) that don't pay well for the amount of work required. Fill in your teaching schedules with those that do.

Check When and How They Pay

Often a virtual university will pay you for the first two-thirds of the class when you start, and the final third after you turn in your final grades for that class. Although some do follow a more traditional method of paying monthly based on your teaching load.

Additionally, some schools pay once a month, and others every two weeks. Why does it matter? It doesn't, once you have got your full teaching load built and running. But when you are working your way up to a livable income stream, it helps to know when and how that money will start trickling in.

Holiday Schedules

Many virtual schools operate just like brick and mortar schools, scheduling classes during the semesters or quarters, and allowing breaks for students and faculty during major holidays. But some of the biggest virtual schools do not. That means if you want those holidays off (or if you want any time off) you have to refuse classes that will run during those times. This can be costly in missed opportunities.

In order to get two weeks off at Christmas when you are teaching nine-week classes, you must start turning down classes nine weeks in advance. This way your teaching schedule will be down to zero by the beginning of Christmas. In the same way, you must start adding classes after your vacation. Since you won't ever get 14 classes beginning at once (no matter how good a teacher you are) you will have to rebuild your teaching load. This takes time too. So you can see how much money you don't earn just to have those two weeks off.

If you are adamant about taking vacations and living a centered, family oriented life, then don't apply to those schools! Stick with the schools that respect their facultys' personal lives and give them holidays. But if building up your savings is the most important thing to you right now, then take every class and work through the holidays. After all, you can do this anywhere there is an internet connection—I spent 2 weeks in Tobago and taught my classes from the hotel lobby computers.

Responsibilities

Additionally, I feel strongly about faculty sticking to teaching, and administration handling, well, the administration of the university. Look at it this way, if you only earn $100 per week teaching one class, do you really want to be spending your time teaching Outlook Express, Whiteboard, eCollege and answering tech questions?

This is really just a way for the school to keep their own costs down by not hiring the staff they need in administration. And those who suffer ultimately are the students-- because their teachers are too busy playing tech support to teach them. Try to stick with schools that have well staffed tech support with 24/7 contact. After all, they don't have to pay for things like leases, electricity, heat, janitorial services, property taxes and all the other overhead that comes with brick and mortar schools. Even their instructors pay for their own offices (in your home) so they need to at least maintain their internet equipment and IT personnel.

What should you be responsible for? You should be responsible for teaching—making sure your students understand what is expected of them. Teaching the concepts in each class and providing additional materials to help students understand these concepts. Providing qualitative, timely feedback on their assignments, encouraging, cajoling, and creating a good learning atmosphere in your classes.

You should also be responsible for knowing everything that is in your syllabus, checking out all external links to make sure they work before classes start, reporting problems with materials used in the class, and answering all questions happily and thoroughly.

That is what teaching is all about, and that doesn't change just because you never look your students in the eye.

Class Size

Most classes I teach are built at 20 students. That means, student schedulers try to enroll a maximum of 20 students in each class. However, I rarely have 20 students stay the entire length of the class. Attrition is very high in

online classes where it is easy to come to
class – and just as easy to miss it.

Introductory classes are always built high and
lose nearly half their students by the end of
the class. However, the more advanced classes
are likely to have students who are more experienced in taking online classes, and more
committed to getting their degree. These classes
will probably not have as many students to start
out with, but are more likely to keep what they
do have.

Either way, you will have a lot of students and
need to keep on top of your grading. Online
classes generally have many small assignments
each week that you need to grade. This is to
make up for the fact that you never see your
students face to face. The online involvement
consists of posting to discussions and the ex-
change of assignments and qualitative feedback from instructors. So keep involved with your
students and they will keep involved in the class.

Contrary to popular opinion, online classes are
not just a new-tech version of correspondence
courses. Anyone who has spent much time chatting online, sending emails and discussing ideas

in newsgroups understands how very rewarding
and connected this kind of relationship can be.
Friends are made, lives are changed. Relation-
ships can be formed even if all you ever see
are words on a screen. But all that is up to the
leader of the group. And that, baby, is you!

Contact with Students

Classes are considered either synchronous
(everyone meets at the same time for a live chat
session) or asynchronous (no requirements about
when to log on to the class) or a combination
of both.

Synchronous

If you like interacting with your students you
will probably really enjoy synchronous teaching. Live chat sessions utilize software like AIM,
where all students and the teacher log on at
the prescribed time and "discuss" that week's
topics. I truly enjoy live chat sessions, since
class dynamics develop more quickly when
we are all writing to each other at the same
time. Although it may seem at first like it will
be absolute chaos, you'll find that it isn't that
hard to conduct a symposium this way at all.

The only problem with chat sessions is that ev-

erybody has to be available at the same time
– which takes away a bit from the advantages
of online learning. The alternative is a purely
asynchronous teaching environment. In this
style, there is no real-time chatting. All conversations are held on threads in a newsgroup.

Asynchronous

Asynchronous classes never meet in real time.
That means, you might not ever be online at
the same time as your student. So all interactions
(posting and answering questions) have a
lag time.

This has its good and bad points. The bad is that
sometimes students (and teachers) become
frustrated by having to wait to get the answers to
their questions. Especially if the question is badly
worded, and the answer is just a request for
clarification.

The good part is that you always have time to
think through exactly what you want to say. You
are never put on the spot like a live class teacher.
You have time to write and revise your answer,
or do a little research if you need clarification
yourself!

But it is harder to keep the conversation moving and keep students involved in an all-asynchronous environment. You, as the facilitator, are responsible for keeping the conversations going in the right direction. You'll need a lot more posting and comments that prompt further discussions.

You might be required to write your own discussion questions that encourage students to think about and interact with the materials from that week, or you might have prescribed discussion questions to work with. Either way, you will be required to post a minimum amount of substantive teaching posts for a number of days each week. And students will be required to reply substantively a minimum amount of times per week.

Office Hours

Finally, the third way you will interact with students is direct contact via office hours. Again, each school has their own methods and requirements for this. One school I work for requires that I hold office hours four hours a day, four days per week, at a specified time. That means during those hours I need to be available by phone and actively monitoring the newsgroups to answer questions.

Another school requires that I have only two scheduled office hours per week, but during that time I must be available for live chat on AIM.

Which you prefer will obviously depend on your personality and schedule. If you want to teach at many schools and optimize your income, you should be prepared to do all of them.

Class Assignment Limits

Most schools limit the number of classes you may be assigned at a time or per quarter. For many this limit is two at a time, or four per quarter. The conceit is that we are all professionals working full-time all day long, and that we just do this in our "spare time."

The truth is that most full-time professionals would never have the time or inclination to spend their evening teaching online classes. Most of us are relying on this income for our survival. That's why it is essential that you be teaching for many schools at once. Remember, in the new economy, companies feel no responsibility toward their employees. So employees need to be looking out for themselves.

Unions

At the time of this writing, I am not aware of any unions for online teachers, although all other public school teachers from nursery school to graduate school have unions to ensure fair hiring, firing and compensation packages. As recently as 2006, the adjuncts at New York University voted to bring in union representation, and the adjuncts at The New School in NYC are presently in negotiations with union representation.

But of the online schools, only Kaplan University faculty ever actively attempted to form a union, and that unfortunately for them, failed. Most online schools consider their faculty to be merely facilitators or worse. They have no bargaining power and no say in how any part of their departments or universities are run. At the University of Phoenix, 90% of the faculty are adjuncts, which means that input from the content experts and teachers themselves into how that university is structured and run is nill.

With the many bright, educated teachers out there eager to work online, these colleges and universities have the freedom to treat their faculty like Walmart employees. And many do, because no matter how badly they treat them, there are

always dozens more adjuncts ready and willing
to take their place.

Faculty generally have no health, vacation, or
benefit plans. What they do have are entirely
inadequate (Kaplan University provides up to
$2000 worth of health insurance per year; UOP
has a pre-tax 401K that employees can con-
tribute to, but contributes no matching funds).
There is no job security, even less than in other
employment-at-will companies. When you are a
permanent, full-time employee for a company,
even though that is still at-will, there is a solid
measure of loyalty between employer and employee. Not so at a school where loyalty lasts only
as long as your 5.5 week contract--after which
you may never hear from that school again
no matter how well you performed your job.

Until there are enough schools in this business
to keep most adjuncts employed, or these
teachers form collective bargaining groups
like their full-time, brick and mortar brethren,
the power to hire and fire at whim will stay entirely with the schools. Pay will be very, very
low, and adjuncts will remain responsible for
their own health and retirement. For this reason, I believe any attempts to create unions

for these faculty, just like the unions that ensure the benefits and employment of full-time brick and mortar faculty, should be encouraged.

3

Maximizing Your Income

Okay, now we've got all the generalities out of the way, let's get down to the nitty-gritty. You want to know how to make 100K or more teaching from your living room (or bedroom, or patio, or rooftop, or pool side) don't you? Yep, I absolutely positively make that much.

The way to do it is to teach a lot of classes at once. Sounds obvious, but without a system

you'll never manage. Believe me, I spent years
working out this system and building to this income level. Now you get the benefit of my trial
and errors. (Boy O'boy were there errors.)

Diversify Your Portfolio

First off, it is essential that you be teaching for
more than one university or college at a time.
Diversify, brother! Just like in your financial portfolio, you need a diverse group of schools in your
teaching portfolio. You need several schools from
which you regularly get teaching assignments.

Teach More Than One Subject

You need to teach more than a single subject,
and you need to always be expanding the
classes you are qualified to teach. This way,
when one school folds, you are not out of a job.
(Hey, remember the Internet bubble? Don't
want a repeat of that, do you?) And when a
school merges with another and changes their
limit on teaching assignments, you can hit up a
different school to fill in the gaps. When you find
yourself on the outs with some Instructional Specialist in one school, you can minimize contact
with that company and maximize it elsewhere.

In this new economy, fluidity is essential. So make

sure you don't get locked into any one school permanently, for all your income. Just like playing the stock market, in this job market you want to diversify. Here's how you do that. . . .

Accept Every Class Offered

At least to begin with, you want to be the teacher faculty schedulers can always turn to. You need to be the reliable one that will take a class two hours before it is scheduled to start, or two weeks in because the other teacher was rushed to the hospital.

Qualify to Teach English and Math

In order to be at the top of the scheduler's list, you also need to be qualified to teach many different classes. High priority are math and English classes, because all entering students must complete a certain number of credit hours in order to go on to their majors. Since every student must take math and English, schools need a lot of teachers for those subjects (which is a good thing, considering all the English majors out there looking for work).

The other thing to do is always sign up for and complete the offered seminars. No matter what they are, they will help you with teach-

ing, and many of them will qualify you to teach
now subjects. As I already mentioned, the more
subjects you qualify to teach, the more likely
you are to get new assignments. And if you
always accept assignments . . . well, you will
be earning your $10K per month in no time!

Create Your Own Best Teaching Schedule

Okay, now some of you are saying you don't
really want to do this full time. That actually, just
$50k a year is enough to live happily on. So fine,
nobody says you have to teach 14 classes at a
time. You can teach just two, or five, or however
many fit your own best teaching schedule. If you
only need a small income stream to support you
and your "real" work (e.g. music, art, writing)
then schedule as many classes as you can easily teach in 20 hours a week and stick with that.

The only thing you need to watch out for is that
you don't let any one school lapse. If you've
taken the time to apply to and be hired to teach
at three schools, then make sure you always
teach something at those three schools. Many
universities will only keep you active for up to
one year without teaching a class. After that,
you have to reapply. So teach that one class
a year at the school that doesn't pay much

and is a pain in the a&& just so you have something to fall back on if the really money-bags
school suddenly trims your teaching schedule.

The System is Everything
The next chapter is where I teach you how
to optimize your teaching skills. Let me intro-
duce that chapter here by saying that the
system you develop is your key to success in
this business. You must create (and stick with)
a schedule and system that takes as much
of the busy work out of this job as possible.

If you spend hours totaling up weekly points
and posting evaluations, then you have a bad
system. If grading papers moves like molas-
ses, your system doesn't work. If it takes you
all day Saturday (your day off) to complete
the grading that you couldn't get done during the previous week, then you need to ana-
lyze your system and see how it is failing you.
I can't tell you how to create your own system. I
can only show you mine. You may adopt it com-
pletely (no copyright infringement) or you may
adopt some parts and dump other parts. Or you
might just use it as inspiration to create your own.

Keep streamlining that system

Ono last caveat, if you aren't always thinking of ways to streamline your work and improve your system so you can get more
done, better, in less time, then you don't
take the value of a system seriously enough.
Earn $100K a year—make a good system.

In academia you rarely hear about optimizing
systems or improving output. That's because
this is one of the last bastions of the secure,
life-time employment. Professors used to start
teaching at universities right out of graduate
school, and keep teaching there until they
were tenured, then stayed on teaching until
they were so old that no student could understand them anymore – and then they got to
retire on a great income and keep teaching
part time just so they wouldn't get bored.

Well, that was the old economy. Now that we
have the new economy, everything is about
productivity, fluidity, and looking out for yourself (rather than hoping your company will look
out for you). Lucky us. Well, suck it up, buttercup
and face reality. If your company isn't loyal to
you, then you be loyal to you. That means always thinking about where you will be working

next week, next month, next year; always shaking the tree looking for the next job, next contract, next teaching assignment. Saving your own Keogh or 401k for retirement, and worrying about your own health care and investments.

Even the great old ivory towers of academia are going this direction with the explosion of new for-profit schools and the newly discovered mother load of adult students wanting to take classes and earn their degrees in their spare time, online. If your university hasn't started teaching online classes yet, it will (and it's behind in the game).

So you need to learn how to work successfully in this new environment. Instead of getting a cushy teaching job where you teach 5 classes a semester, always have the summers off, and get paid bupkis, now you need to think about teaching as many classes as you can possibly handle by teaching smart, teaching at multiple schools, and finally earning the income good teachers deserve.

Teach Smart Not Hard!
Is teaching smart the same thing as shirking your students? Not a chance, kiddo! Teach-

ing smart is all about putting the focus on the teaching part of your job, and streamlining all the rule-following and busy-work part of your job. That makes teaching smart a win-win for all involved: students, teachers, and universities.

Optimizing Your Teaching

The key to making a living teaching online full-time is to manage your time. Fill your portfolio with classes that don't require a 30hr a week commitment each. (Would you teach for $9 an hour? Less than minimum wage in many states?)

And get organized. Organization is the key to streamlining your teaching. And that's the only way to handle more than a handful of classes at a time.

The major players in this industry use everything from their own online, proprietary system, to commercial systems like Web CT and eCollege, to plain old newsgroups accessed by Outlook Express. You should learn to be comfortable in all these platforms so that you can easily jump from class to class, subject to subject on a daily basis.

Here are the Big Four:
University of Phoenix
Axia College
Kaplan University
Art Institute Online

I'll take you through them one at a time so you can see how they operate and how they compare to each other.

Teaching at The University of Phoenix
The University of Phoenix still uses Outlook Express for all of its online courses, although at this writing they are transitioning over to a proprietary, web-based version of Outlook Express. As this is one of the largest employers for online instructors, you must learn to be proficient in this envi-

ronment. I've been teaching for UOP for years so I've got plenty of tips to share with you!

Teaching Load. Faculty generally teach 1-2 at a time, although, if you are in a department where they are in need of facilitators, you can be scheduled up to four at a time. (I have heard, in the faculty chatroom, that some have had six at a time.)

Once you become a full-fledged Facilitator (UOP refuses to use either the Professor or the Adjunct titles) you will be contacted periodically by the course schedulers from the departments in which you have been approved to teach. They will offer you classes, and if you accept you will be sent a provisional contract via email. (Provisional, because the class can be cancelled at any time up until the day it begins.)

Length of class. UOP classes last five-weeks. They are accelerated courses and the workload for students as well as facilitators is heavy. Classes run from Tuesday through Monday, with Monday being the last day of the UOP week. That means Monday night is when you set up all your classes for the start of the new week.

Holidays. UOP gives a one week break at Christmas and Thanksgiving. Other one day holidays are not observed.

Technology. UOP has a website for faculty and students, but doesn't utilize it much. Most of the real work happens on Outlook Express (OE).

Class set-up. All classes take place in Newsgroups. Any single class at UOP will consist of four kinds of newsgroups:
1. The Main newsgroup which is like the classroom
2. The Course Materials newsgroup, which is where you post any materials you want students to read
3. The Chatroom newsgroup, which is like the student union building where students can chat about things that are not class related, and
4. Four Team newsgroups. At UOP the teaching model uses the dreaded teamwork approach. Which means that each class is divided into 2–4 teams and each team is responsible for completing several assignments.

Participation. UOP requires that you post 4-5 messages in the main newsgroup, on five days per week.

Graded assignments. There are usually 1-2 small assignments each week, and one large paper. All graded assignments must be returned to students within seven days of the end of the week, and each week you must also post a weekly evaluation that includes the points earned so far in the class. UOP also has an online grade book for faculty to use.

Office hours. There are no required office hours at UOP.

Teaching flexibility. Although all courses are pre-designed and packaged, and some even have course web pages where students can find the reading and supplemental materials to download, the facilitator has a fairly free hand to modify the course, write his/her own DQs, and provide any supplementary materials they choose as long as they meet the weekly course objectives.

Teaching at Axia College

Axia College is a new venture of UOP, launched in the fall of 2004. It is an attempt to funnel incoming students through the equivalent of a 2 year community college before passing them on to the UOP staff and faculty. Axia college emphasizes hand holding and extra-friendly

facilitation. Students are often barely qualified to be in a college class at all, so expect to
move slowly and practice patience explaining
everything. You are the first contact for these
students in an online college world, and they
need you to walk them through the course.

Teaching Load. The load has changed frequently as Axia fills its roster with available,
trained faculty. At this writing, facilitators may
teach no more than four classes at a time.

Once you become a full-fledged facilitator you
will be contacted periodically by the course
schedulers from the departments in which you
have been approved to teach. They will offer
you classes. You will be sent a link to sign onto a
website where you can accept or decline the
offer. (Provisional, because the class can be
cancelled at any time up until the day it begins.)

Length of class. Axia classes last nine-weeks.
Although still technically accelerated courses,
they move quite a bit slower for these newbie
students.

Holidays. Axia College has just granted faculty and students a one-week break at Christ-

mas. Before 2006, there were no breaks at all
for any holidays. One-day holidays are observed merely by cancelling office hours.

Technology. Axia classes are all online, including
all readings and assignments for students. All texts
are etexts except some literature and humanities
classes. Class also takes place on a proprietary
web-based newsgroup that simulates Outlook
Express. It is awkward and full of bugs. Luckily,
you still have the option to use OE to access the
newsgroups for this class--which I recommend.

Class Set-up. The technical set up for Axia
includes:
1. A main newsgroup that is like the classroom
2. A chatroom newsgroup for students to use
in off-topic discussions
3. A course-materials newsgroup where you
can post any supplementary course materials for
students
4. And an individual newsgroup (ING) for each
student where they can correspond with you in
private, and post their assignments and get
their evaluations.

Participation. Axia also requires that you post 3-4
messages in the main newsgroup, on four

days per week during a participation week.
Since participation weeks alternate with work
weeks, you only have to do this every-other
week during the course.

Graded assignments. There are usually 1-2 small
assignments each week, and one large paper.
The small assignments must be graded within
24 hours during the week, or during your next
office hours if it is the weekend. (Weekends
are Friday and Saturday at Axia, since Sunday is a workday there.) The big assignments
must be graded within seven days of posting.

Office hours. Axia requires that you be online four
days a week, Sunday through Thursday, from
4pm-8pm as your office hours. Students must be
able to reach you via posts in their newsgroups,
email and phone calls during your office hours.

During this time you are supposed to be cruising the newsgroups looking for questions posted.
This is a huge time commitment, especially if you
only have a few Axia classes. Since the rule is
that you must answer any questions that were
posted during your office hours by the end of
those same office hours, it's a better use of your
time to check in during the last half hour of

your office hours and answer questions then.

Teaching flexibility. There is very little flexibility for facilitators at Axia. All class modules are
created for you, and you are not allowed to
change anything. Even the discussion questions
are pre-written, and sometimes pretty boring.
But you can always post additional questions
to spur the conversations. All grade points are
preassigned and cannot be changed. The late
assignment policy is fixed and also unchange-
able, and there is no extra credit allowed.

Teaching At Kaplan University

In my opinion, Kaplan University is the best of the
three big for-profit, online universities. KU imitates
the infrastructure of a traditional, on-ground
university with colleges, deans, assistant deans,
departments, chairs and assistant chairs for
each department. This allows all faculty a clear
understanding of the hierarchy at the school,
and a better grip on how everything works.

Approximately 1/3 of each department is made
up of full-time faculty members, with the other
two-thirds adjuncts. This means there is more
continuity for the departments and the students. Adjuncts have the added incentive of

applying for those full-time positions when they come vacant (although this is not frequent).

Once you have completed the training and mentoring, you will likely be assigned the full class limit each term, and can usually count on teaching those classes every term.

Teaching load. Adjuncts teach a total of two classes per term. This used to be three classes, each built at about 15 students. However, in December of 2006 KU implimented new limits and teaching requirements. So now classes are built at 25 students, and adjuncts are limited to 2 courses at a time. (Cute, huh? As if we couldn't figure out that we're teaching the same number of students for 1/3d less money now.) At last report, KU was reconsidering their 2 class limit for adjuncts.

Full time faculty teach five per term and have other administrative responsibilities.

Length of class. Classes last 10 weeks. Each week is a "unit" in the class; each unit starts on Wednesday and ends on the following Tuesday.

Holidays. There is a one-week break between

each class, and one week at Christmas. Other one-day holidays are observed by cancelling office hours or seminars if they fall on that day.

Technology. KU uses eCollege. All classes, reading, exercises and the grade book are on the KU website. In fact, everything you need to teach the class is prepared for you in advance. All you have to do at the start of the class is upload your syllabus and welcome message.

Class setup. Each week (Unit) of the class is a section of the class website. Each section is divided into readings, exercises, discussions and projects. Papers are submitted to an online "drop box" that delivers them to the teacher's webpage inbox. All comments and grading can be done through this website, including the use of a really spectacular grade book that keeps track of all grades, averages and comments on each student's assignments.

Participation. Participation has also recently changed. Faculty are now required to post 8-10 separate times, spread evenly throughout the week on the discussion webpage for each unit. They must also conduct a one-hour synchronous seminar with the student, in which

that week's lesson is taught. And keep 2 hours
of live office time using AIM each wook.

Graded assignments. Discussions, seminars
and the weekly projects are graded each
week for each student. The new turnaround
time for grading projects is 5 days, seminars
must be graded within 48 hours.

Office hours. Faculty are required to have
two hours per week in which they can be
reached via Instant Messenger as their office
hours, and answer any emails within 24 hours.

Teaching flexibility. All classes are thoroughly
developed and vetted by all faculty. Substantive changes must be approved by the
lead faculty for that course. Minor changes that do not require changing any assignment point values are allowed.

Teaching at Art Institute Online
AIO is a new venture for the Art Institute, an on-
ground for profit school with campuses around
the country. Because it has recently launched,
the infrastructure is still in flux, and classes are
often not QC'd and sometimes difficult to work
with. However, because the students are well-

qualified and generally also take on-ground classes, the caliber of assignments is quite a bit better than some of the more established online schools, as is the caliber of student.

Teaching Load. Adjuncts may teach no more than two classes at a time, and full-time faculty no more than four at a time.

Length of class. AIO classes last five and a half weeks. They are very accelerated, and really do try to cram a full term (or more) worth of work into those 5.5 weeks.

Holidays. AIO schedules classes around the usual holidays, so that you won't be working Christmas morning.

Technology. AIO uses eCollege. Although at this point their grasp of the software is sketchy. You're likely to know more about the functions of eCollege than they do, if you've used it before.

Class Set-up. AIO claims all courses are turn-key ready for the faculty. However, in my experience every course requires *substantial* work to make it usable for yourself and the students. The good news is that you are allowed to make those usability changes if you want to take the time.

Participation. AIO participation requirements
are almost abusive of faculty time. You are
required to post 20% of all the posts in every
thread in your classroom, or about one post
for every five student posts. Since there is an
average of 2 discussion threads and 4 assignments each week, that's a lot of posting.

Your posts are also required to be quite substantive and content-based. So no filling in
with any "good work, nice job" kind of posts.

Recently implimented is the new requirement
that you respond to each and every posted
assignment on the threads within 48 hours of
posting, as well as grade those assignments in
the grade book at the end of each week.

Each week there are 2-3 discussion questions,
3-4 additional assignment discussion threads, a
teacher's questions thread and a general question thread. You are required to monitor and
post to all of these, 5 out of 7 days a week.

Additionally, classes are built at 20 students, so
that you might have 250-300 posts from your

students each week on all these threads, which would required you to post between 45-55 solid, substantive, discussion furthering posts every week.

Now, think about it: the more you encourage student discussion the more work you have to do in order to keep that 1:5 ratio of posts. It won't take the faculty member long to realize that more students posting requires more faculty posting. In fact, if the faculty uses the very effective Socratic method for online discussions, where every post includes a new question prompting new thinking and replies, it is a mathematical impossibility that the faculty will *ever* meet the required 20% level.

Consciously or subconsciously that knowledge is going to be reflected in the number of questions and open-ended messages faculty post to students. AIO might find themselves rethinking this policy.

Graded assignments. AIO also over-does it with the assignment load. There are between 3-6 assignments per week, which include a full paper, a quiz that must be manually graded, and 2-3 smaller assignments in addition to the discussion questions.

It's my experience that when students are required to complete that many graded assignments each week, they become overwhelmed
by the work load. They either drop out altogether,
or end up doing such a slap-dash job on the
assignments that they learn nearly nothing.

Additionally, AIO insists on substantive, de-
tailed feedback for each of these assignments, including the quiz while giving Faculty
just 2.5 days from the end of each week to
grade all assignments for that week. The re-
sult can only be, that faculty will also do a
slap-dash job in their grading each week.

This is a classic case of quantity over quality.

Office hours. There are no required office
hours at AIO.

Teaching flexibility. There is very little flexibility for facilitators at AIO. All class modules are
created for you, although you may make
small changes to the presentation of the
material, none of the material itself can be
changed. Even the discussion questions are
pre-written, and sometimes pretty boring.

All grade points and grade rubrics are preassigned and cannot be changed. There is no
stated late assignment policy at this point,
so you can at least set that standard.

The Four-Part System

Part of the drawback of online universities is that nobody ever meets face to face. I have never met any of the students or administration that I've worked with during the 3000 classes I've taught online.

That's not to say I don't know them pretty well, email them constantly, and stay in touch with them daily. But there remains

that residual sense among employers that
if they are not leaning over your shoul-
der minute-by-minute watching everything
you do, that you might be "slacking off."

So online universities have come up with
their own unique way of checking-up on
their teachers. They create a whole bunch
of rules of operation that teachers must follow, and a whole group of people whose
sole job is to check up on the teachers to
see that they are following those rules.

The rules look something like this:

• Faculty must post at least 4 substantive
messages on 5 out of 7 days each week.

• Housekeeping messages are not considered
substantive.

• Grades on checkpoints must be posted by
the end of the next office hours.

• Grades on assignments must be posted within
five days of the due date of the assignment.

• Weekly evaluations must be posted within seven days of the end of the week.

• All evaluations must include qualitative and quantitative feedback, including substantive comments about how a student is progressing in the class.
Etc . . . .

Additionally, these rules are slightly different from school to school, and they change quite frequently. What's a dedicated online professor to do? You have to use the Four-Part System.

These rules are the ways universities have invent-ed to help them feel that they are getting their money's worth out of their online faculty. The ones that work at home, that they never, ever see. Don't get me wrong, I like these rules. It is important that you stay involved in your classes, that you discuss course subjects in a substantive way, that you give feedback quickly and that it actually tell students how to improve their work. I think every teacher should follow these rules.

The only problem is, like any set of rules, some-times the rules themselves become more impor-tant that the intent behind the rules. Sometime it becomes more important to administrators that you post four messages on five days a week, than that the content of those messages be intelligent and enlivening, or that the dynamics be challenging and vivid. That's when rules and teaching seem to get in each other's way.

But hey, I am a pragmatist. These are the rules. You will have to follow them. So instead of moaning and groaning (or at least after I moaned and groaned a bit) I started developing a system that would ensure that I follow all the rules exactly, and that the students got the quality of teaching that I am capable of giving. That should be your goal too.

You can see how important is must be, then, to have a system that helps you keep track of when you have a teaching responsibility, and that ensures that you follow all these requirements without spending every waking hour doing your online classes. Well, that's what I have . . . so read on!

The first thing you will need to do once you've got a class to teach, is make yourself a system that ensures you get everything done each week that needs to be done, and that you are utilizing all the available resources to help make your job easier. My system consists of four parts: a calendar, the perfect online tone, course materials prepared in advance, and a number of online utilities that really make my job easier.

Create & Use a Teaching Calendar

It is hugely important that you set yourself a schedule for getting everything done each week – and that you stick to it. This will take some work, and I can't just give you a schedule, because every teaching load is different, and each school you teach for will require different participation from you. So don't worry if you don't have the perfect schedule the first week – this is an ongoing project.

Here is my schedule, so you have an example. I've been slowly developing this one over the years, incorporating new requirements as I am assigned new classes at new schools. It's expandable, so that I can accommodate a full load of classes (14 – 20) and contractible, so if I'm down to just 7 classes, I spend an equivalently less time working them, giving me more time to do other things – like write this little book.

Weekly Calendar of Responsibilities

SUNDAY

A bulk of my classes start on Monday morning, which means that I have to upload all materials for the new week Sunday night.

One of my colleges requires me to have office hours on Sunday night (bluck!) so I consider Sunday my first day of the week. I finish up anything that needed to get done the previous week, and set up my classes for the new week. I upload all new course materials, change the names of my classes to reflect their new week (see the discussion about naming classes in OE below) and subscribe to any new classes I have been assigned. Sunday can be a very busy day, or a fairly light day, depending on how well I've stuck to my teaching

schedule the week before.

MONDAY

This is the first day of the week for many of the classes I teach. If I'm starting new classes, this is the day I check in and say hello to everyone (I like to make a personal hello to each of my new students.) Since many classes had to turn in their weekly assignments Sunday night, this is the day I go through and start grading those assignments.

Grading assignments might take up to two days to complete, and it's best to get started early, since I can't post the weekly evaluations until those grades are done.

I also have some classes that end on this day. So I have to upload new materials for their next week, subscribe to new classes for that school, etc.

I make sure to read through all the newsgroups and post my minimum of four substantive messages in the main newsgroups. This is the day to get student inspired to discuss the topics of that week. I post all my additional materials for that week on Monday, to spark some good discussions for the rest of the week.

It's a lot easier for me and the students to meet participation requirements when there is a great conversation going. It's my job to get it going.

The last thing I do before I log off at the end of my office hours is to scan through each newsgroup looking for questions that need to be answered.

TUESDAY

I am still probably grading weekly assignments today. Once I get all the grading done, I can post my weekly evaluations. This just involves totalling up each student's points for the previous week, adding it to their personal grade sheet, and either sending or posting that grade sheet to them. (Some classes have individual newsgroups where I post these, others have grade books that automatically record the grades for me and show the students, and still others I have to email the grades to.)

I make sure to post my minimum messages in each newsgroup today and the last thing I do before I log off for the day is scan the newsgroups for questions.

WEDNESDAY

I will finish up the weekly

ovaluations today. Best practice is to have the evaluations completed and posted within four days of the end of the week. The faster the students see feedback, the faster they can incorporate that into their next assignment.

By this day students are working on new assignments and checkpoints in some of my courses, so I like to be finished with all the grading from the previous week so I can focus on the new assignments.

I make sure to post my minimum messages for that day and before I log off check for questions.

Because I also have several classes that require one-hour live seminars, I will teach one of these on three night of the week. There isn't much to prepare in advance, because I've already created all the PowerPoint presentations for those seminars in advance.

THURSDAY

I will have checkpoints to grade today. Those are small, weekly assignments that require a quick turn-around. Since I keep grading rubrics for all assignments, organized by the week, I can simply copy and paste these into my messages and fill in the comments that pertain to each individual student.

I will have another live seminar to teach tonight, as well as having to remember to post my participation posts in all my classes.

The last thing I do before I turn off the computer is check for questions.

FRIDAY

This is my day off! I always find at least one day a week that I don't have to sign on at all, and I make sure my computer is off on that day. Because one of the schools I work for requires that I never take two days off in a row, I never have two days off a week. But I make up for that with only working half days on some days (like Saturday)

You will never be able to do this job long-term if you can't find at least one day off a week to take a break. So figure out when that can be, and keep it sacrosanct!

SATURDAY

Today I have to grade papers for several classes that end on Thursday. Because I only have 2.5 days to get the grades done for that school, I spend most of my Saturday morning grading those assignments. Since

I don't have any office hours or teach any seminar on Saturday, I am finished once the grades are done.

SUNDAY

Here we are again! If I've stuck to my schedule, I don't have any papers to grade today, nor any weekly evaluations to do. I probably do have some checkpoints to grade. Anything that was turned in Thursday, Friday or Saturday has to be graded today.

Also, many classes have to be set up for the new week, and if I have new classes starting on Monday, I need to set those up today too.

That's my all important calendar. When I stick to it, I meet all my requirements for all the different schools I work for. When I don't, I get a testy little message from one of the "Instructional Specialists" pointing out that although I posted 10 substantive messages on Thursday, I only posted three substantive messages on Wednesday, and so I have not fulfilled my teaching requirements. These messages are an annoyance, especially to anyone who takes teaching seriously (and has a tendency not to take process all that seriously). But they are a reality. So if you want to avoid them, write a good calendar for yourself that incorporates everything you need to do for all your schools each week, and stick with it!

Cultivate the Perfect Online Tone

The tone you use online in emails to associates and students, and in your posts in classes to students, is the key to your success in this business overall. It can take some getting used to, if you are new to communicating entirely in print. Most of us learned our social skills from face-to-face interactions. We know how to see and project friendly, open body language. We use inflections in our voices to convey concern, humor, amiability. But none of that survives the move to print.

Once you find yourself conversing entirely through your words on the screen, you might feel lost in a void of expressions you cannot convey accurately. Jokes fall flat, satire is lost in translation, and the most neutral of emails is received as a condemnation or worse by a student in fear for their grade. Here are a few rules to help you avoid the pitfalls of "bad tone" online. Learn from my mistakes!

Never use sarcasm. That's certainly the first and foremost. Many people don't get sarcasm in f2f encounters. So why would you expect them to get it in a post or email? It is dangerous, leads to tearful, angry replies, and is almost impossible to recover from. Just avoid it altogether.

Emoticons are your friend, but not your savior. If you thought popping a smiley face at the end of a crushing sentence would save the tone, you were wrong. Until students (and associates) really get to know your online style, and establish a rapport in print with you, no amount of smileys in the world will help a sentence that is less that polite or jovial.

If in doubt, go overboard with the compliments. But only with compliments! Start every critique with a compliment and end every criticism with a compliment. Never say "No." Think of a way to say no so that you sound like you're saying yes, (Sometimes I start with "Yes, but . . . ") Make your nicest comments even nicer. Don't worry about sounding gushy. You won't, you'll sound supportive.

Use extra exclamation points. In online speak, the exclamation point has a different meaning from in traditional print usage. Online it literally denotes cheerfulness. Use it a lot! Use it more than a lot! Make your college English teacher sick with the number of exclamation points you use!!! It might be bad punctuation but it is good tone online.

Never use ALL CAPS, bold, or l33tspeak. All caps are what newbies to the web use before they've figured out that it looks like you're shouting when you write in all caps. It feels like a slap in the face to the person reading the message. It's hard for the best of us to recover from that emotional jolt, even once we figure out that the author didn't know they were shouting.

NEVER USE ALL CAPS! (See what I mean?)

Bold implies the kind of emphasis that the exclamation mark does in traditional print. It is very strong, and should be used with great care. I suggest never using it at all. It's hard enough to be sure people read your notes with the level, polite tone that they were written.

And all that short hand that people have learned to use while typing on their phones with their thumbs? It's cute. Save it for your phone; don't use it in class. There are still only a limited number of people who know what the most basic of those abbreviations mean, and those that don't know will feel lost and embarrassed that they don't. Most of them won't ask, because they think they should know. So they will go on getting more and more frustrated by the "secret" comments that everyone understands but them. (It took me two years teaching online seminars before I figured out that BRB didn't mean my student just burped at me.) It's hard enough to convey a clear message with this medium without adding that kind of confusion.

Prepare Your Course Materials In Advance

This is really the best part of teaching classes online. You have plenty of time to research and develop all kinds of interesting materials, as well as prepare all your required materials well in advance.

Make Folders for each class—If you are an organizational freak like me, you will set up folders for each class, and folders for each week of each class (and if you're a real freak you could have a folder for each day of each class in each week) and put your prepared materials there. Then when it is time to upload each day, everything is already done.

Prepare all substantive posts and additional materials ahead of time and save them in your folders. Of course this takes substantial prep time. But you can even prepare in advance all the substantive posts that need to be posted 5 out of 7 days each week, so you're not sitting in front of 14 classes every day sweating out something intelligent to say for the umpteenth time about Greek columns.

Save your best comments and lectures in your
folders to reuse in other classes. As you complete each week of each course, you can
pull those particularly brilliant comments you
made to the class into your folders and reuse
them for the next class – not something brick
and mortar teachers can do very easily!

Write grade rubrics for every assignment.
These should include the requirements for
each individual assignment, the title of the
assignment, and the day it is due. That way,
as you grade you can copy and paste this
rubric into your message, and fill in the comments for that student. (Better yet, save
some of your best comments on the grade
rubrics. Then as you do the grading you can
adapt what you've written for each individual student. But you don't have to rein-
vent the wheel for ever paper you grade.)

Paste the title of the assignment and the
points received into the subject line of the
message. I do this especially in Axia College
classes where I have individual newsgroups

(INGs) for each student. Then when I total up the points for the week, I only have to scan through the INGs looking for my posts with the points. It saves me from opening each post again, scrolling to the bottom, and looking for the point total I already assigned.

Post weekly evaluations in the assignment newsgroup. Rather than save any of this on your hard drive (think how fast your hard drive will fill up) or trying to save it in your "save emails" box (again, fills up too fast) save it to the school's server. Not the tiny bit of the server that has been allotted to you, but in the very classroom where you are teaching.

At UOP there is an Assignments newsgroup that students can post to, but only the teacher can read from. I post all my weekly evaluations for each student in there. That way I can easily find every evaluation I've sent to a student from that class, and it is archived along with the class by the school rather than by me.

At Axia College, evaluations are posted in the INGs, so the same system applies. And at Kaplan, there is unending space on the "sent emails" server, so I always have a record of evaluations in that folder, on their server.

Write all your comments in the newsgroup or comments box on the grade sheet. You will be amazed how much time this save! When you write your comments on the paper, you have to download the paper, save it to a file (name it correctly with the student's name, write the comments, save the file, attach it to a post and upload it. All that extra time and effort, just so the comment can be at the top or the bottom of the paper? Crazy! Of course, if you are teaching a writing class, and you want to include contextual-ized edits in the paper, then you take the extra time. But I only do contextual edits for one paper per class—certainly not for ev-ery assignment every student turns in.

Use All the Many Online Tools Available

Once you get into this business, you find that there are a whole lot of other people in the business too. And they all have gone to a lot of trouble and expense to create tools that make your job easier. Wasn't that nice of them? So use all those great tools out there. Here are some of the best ones: The Discovery Website has a section especially for teachers. There are plenty of tutorials for your students, as well as tools for making tests online. These are invaluable for scoring those silly little multiple choice tests that universities love to include in their modules. Don't waste your time scoring a test that can be set to grade itself.

Getting Them to Like You

The key to this job, like any job really, is to get your students, coworkers and the administration to like you. Sometimes this seems to be a snap, and sometimes you run into snafus that you never would have imagined.

Of course, every teacher wants their students to like them. But let's face it, this job isn't about being popular. Nobody that evaluates someone else's work for a living can win a popularity contest with those people—not and keep their integrity.

Yet, somehow we must actually teach our students, maintain a standard for our profession, and be well liked enough by students, supervisors, and the administration at large to keep our jobs. Not such an easy task in this particular industry!

Students

No matter what administration might tell you, your teaching assignments are contingent on whether you receive good reviews from your students. Each college will have a different method for assessing student response to their faculty, but all rely on some kind of student evaluation, usually an online evaluation the student fills out during the second to last week of class.

Now, think about it. You're hired to teach and evaluate the work product of your students. Part of your job is to give genuine, real-world feedback to the learners in your class so that they might strive to work harder, learn more, and be more success-ful in their academic and future careers.

But your student evaluations, and hence your likelihood of getting future teaching assign-ments, hinges on how those same students evaluate you. Did you give someone a B when **they** thought they earned an A? Expect to receive less than stellar marks from that student on your evaluation.

Did you refuse to accept an assignment three weeks past the due date? Watch out for the angry comments that student writes for you.

Did a student take offense because you corrected him in class, asked for bet-ter sources on a paper, insisted that he do the reading. More low marks for you.

Not all students will be this retaliatory, of course. Some will give careful, honest evalu-ations of your performance, just as you give of theirs. That's why the weight that a school puts on student evaluations in your overall performance in this job is so determinative. If the primary indicator of your fitness to teach in the eyes of a University is how well you did on your student evaluations, you can see that there will arise, over a short time, a serious conflict of interest for those faculty.

Give your students high marks, and they give you high marks. They get passing grades and graduate with honors, and you get to keep teaching.

But give your students low marks (even if clearly well earned) and they give you equally low marks. Students drop out of school, schools lose the tuition from those students, and faculty are not asked back to teach again.

Of course, all colleges have student evaluations, and most take them quite seriously. But in for-profit schools, which all these big online Universities are, their revenues depend on keeping students happy and in class. The student is the customer, and you, my dear, are the employee tasked to keep the customer happy.

So how do you do that, while maintaining a grasp on your own ethical values and professional pride? It's a tight rope walk, I am not going to kid you. But here are a few tips that will help.

Explain everything to your students up front. Make sure that if you have late assignment policies and policies for plagiarism, make-up work and extra credit that they are clearly stated in the syllabus, and in several separate places in the class. The point is not just to have something to point to when students want special consideration for their many life's trials and tribulations, but so that they know in the beginning what will fly with you and what will not.

This won't satisfy every student. There will always be someone who feels that they should get special exemptions, or that they can fool you with a well-worded excuse. But for the majority, having it explained clearly in the begining sets them on notice for the whole class. They are less likely to "trust" that you'll accept their work late, or won't check to see if the paper is plagiarized, if you notify them ahead of time that you won't and you will.

When someone does ask for extra time, ex-
plain thoroughly why you will or will not grant
_it_. Remember, these are adult students, and
they are accustomed to getting clear ex-
planations for most things. Simply saying,
"No" won't cut it with them. And you will
come across sounding uncaring. Which is
the kiss of death for the online instructor.

I recommend using language that subtly puts
the blame on administration, or implies that
you'd be somehow cheating the rest of the
students if you made an exception here and
now. "I'd really love to help, and I would if
I could. But I must abide by the rules of the
university. . ." Or "That's just terrible I am so
sorry such an awful thing happened. I would
love to help in any way I can, but of course,
I have to stick with the late policy in the syllabus. But if there is anything else I can do . . . "

Sometimes, all they really want to hear is
that you care.

Use your rubrics for grading. If you have a
good rubric that clearly lays out the per-
centage that various elements of an as-

signment are worth to the total value of that assignment, then you can write quick, pointed notes that inform the student exactly where their papers did not live up to the requirements of the rubric.

Again, the more specific, the better.

> *"Mechanics are worth 20% of this grade. I noticed quite a few spelling errors that you should have caught with a simple run-through of the spell checker. Also, many of your sentences were convoluted and difficult to understand. Watch out for grammatical errors: accept does not have the same meaning as except."*

<u>Never, ever shame or reprimand a student in class</u>. If a student is unruly or making inappropriate comments in the class, you should contact administration immediately and let them handle it. If a student simply states an incorrect answer during a discussion, you need to find a very polite way to contradict them.

> "Wow . . . you made some very good points here, Billy! But remember, child porn is not protected speech. So no one convicted of creating child pornography could argue a First Amendment defense."

*Don't speak in person to a student unless ab-
solutely necessary*. I know, this sounds heartless
and uncaring. But, most schools require you to
document all your conversations with students
and discourage personal calls anyway. And
there is no way to prove what was said (or
not said) in a conversation over the phone.

I prefer that all conversations occur in print,
on the school servers, so there is a record of
all that is said. I know enough about my students to worry about untrue accusations,
and if they are made during a phone call, I
have no record to show they didn't happen.

A record is really the only way to protect
yourself from a student who takes a personal dislike to you and decides to make
your life a living hell. If it's all in print, and
you have remained cool and professional
in all your responses, then the university will
likely take your side in the matter. (But you
will still probably be hit with those lousy student evaluations at the end of the class.)

There is No Free Speech in Online School.
Let me put that another way: everything

you write is recorded and stored. With
the click of a mouse, all your posts, emails
and in some cases live chats that passed
through that school's server can be col-
lated into one large database and re-
viewed by anyone in the administration.

There is no room for error, no place for off-
handed comments or messages that meet
less than your professional standard of communication. You will never be forgiven for
a tetchy remark or a bit of sarcasm at the
expense of student or administration. So
don't be tempted to let your fingers fly!

The greatest difference between online
school and brick and mortar school, and
what I consider the greatest deficit, is that
there can be no free speech when all speech
is recorded and the possibility of review
looms large. This is chilling at its coldest.

In the brick and mortar classroom, discussions can roam from one extreme to the
other freely, since comments begin to
fade nearly as soon as they are spoken.
Generally, students and faculty can ex-

plore ideas and express view points without fear of the university powers stepping in to condemn or silence the speakers.

Not so in a world of database storage. So reconcile yourself to that fact. Whatever you do, keep a professional tongue in your head. Do not be baited into emotional responses to students or administrative staff. When you feel your blood pressure rise, walk away from the computer until it settles back down again. (That's something you can't do in on-ground classrooms.)

If students send spiteful, hate-filled emails to you—and someone at some time will, no matter how lovable you really are—only respond with the exact facts they need for that situation. Just ignore the rest.

Remember, teachers get fired for what they write online; students do not. As long as they pay their tuition, the most belligerent, obnoxious and threatening student can and does stay in the classroom of these for profit schools.

Schedulers

The schedulers should be your best friend—
make it so! They hand out the classes, they
decide who gets cancelled if a class isn't
full enough. They keep short sheets of their
most reliable faculty, who they can call
at a moment's notice if they have a class
un-staffed. You want to be on that list.

Availability

The way to the scheduler's heart is to be
available when she needs you, but not be
bothersome when she doesn't. Again, another
tricky relationship!

Somehow you must remind the scheduler
that you are around and willing (and wanting)
to take another class, without being that
annoying person that is emailing every day
demanding more work.

Don't Nag!

Since most schools have course load limits, you
should be aware if you have reached your limit
or not. Don't bother the scheduler for more
work if your limit has been met. They can't give
it to you.

Be the Go-To-Faculty

But if you know that you could take another class or two, it is perfectly reasonable to drop a quick email to your scheduler to see if anything has come up. Often they do, and if you email at the right time, you'll be the one to get it.

After a few times, the scheduler will start thinking of you as the "Go-To" faculty member and email you first when a last minute class needs a teacher. Always, always accept! This is the best way to ingratiate yourself to that scheduler.

After all, they want to get all the classes assigned to a teacher for that week so they can go home and forget about work. And you want to build up your teaching schedule so you make six figures this year. If you are nice, this can be a win-win situation

Instructional Specialists

The Instructional Specialist (IS) is the term UOP and some other schools reserves for their faculty supervisors.

All materials describing the job of these IS persons make them sound like they are your liaison with the administration. Your port in a storm, your advocate in case of classroom issues. However, they are nothing of the sort and you must not be fooled by the rhetoric. The IS is your boss! She tells you when you have done something wrong, and she expects you to immediately correct and apologize for the error.

You must never, ever irritate the IS, because it is solely due to their good will that you remain in standing at UOP. If you do get on the wrong side of the IS, there are simply too many ways she can build a case against your continued employment to ever prove her wrong.

Remember, this isn't the real world, this is online university. There is no free speech, you cannot resort to any substantive due process. If the Instructional Specialist doesn't like you, then I advise you to start applying to a new school. That said, here are some ways to avoid run-ins with the IS team.

Don't make a student mad at you. Please see section I of this chapter for how to avoid this problem. If you do make a student mad, they can do more than harm you on your evaluations. They can contact their academic advisors, who will contact the IS department. If the IS department feels you have transgressed on university policies, they will suspend your teaching schedule.

Remember, students are customers. Somehow you must keep them happy even while you try to teach them a thing or two.

If you are contacted by IS, respond immediately. Apologize, and fix whatever it was that you did wrong. But please, check their facts. There have been plenty of times that IS has sent me a note about not participating enough in class, only to find that they have miss-calculated. If they are wrong, then you can politely point out how they were wrong. If you were wrong, just apologize and let the issue go.

Follow every posting and grading rule exactly. If grades were to be turned in on Sunday, then make sure they have all been completed by the stroke of midnight on Sunday.

If you are required to post three times, on each of five days of the week, don't assume you can get away with posting 15 messages on just four days that week. You can't.

The key to staying on the good side of IS is scrupulously following the letter of the law. They are not at all concerned with the substantive evaluation of your teaching, only procedural evaluations. So count your posts, get those evaluations in on time, and log in on the right days each week.

Administration

For other schools that are more traditionally arranged, like Kaplan University, your supervisor is your chair or assistant chair. She is more likely to be another faculty member sympathetic to your issues and needs. At Kaplan, the chair is in charge of your department. She wants to keep her faculty happy as well as her students, and so is less likely to take the Nazi approach to supervision.

Also, in these institutions, the hierarchy is transparent so that students, faculty and

administration are all aware of how the
university is run.

Still, you need to remain on good terms not
only within your department, but in the school,
and in the university itself. So professional tone
and carefully constructed notes are required
here as well. Also, don't forget to save copies of all your own emails, especially those to
administration. You never know when you will
need them to support your side in a dispute.

Online Schools & Programs

Here is the most recent and complete list of schools offering online courses and degree programs as of this writing.

As you browse through these schools, make a list of those that you feel are appropriate places to teach. Remember, not all schools will allow you to teach from distant locations. Some are purely online institutions and are more likely to have all online faculty. But some are traditional schools that are just transitioning into the distance learning business. They are likely to take a more traditional look at running their online departments. Which means although you teach online, you do it from their facilities, not your own

Accreditation

All schools listed are accredited, and all have requirements about the kind of degree you will need in order to teach in each of their programs. If you discover that one of the schools listed here does not have proper higher education accreditation, please let us know so we can remove it from this list.

Degree Requirements

In general, you must have an M.A. to teach in any undergraduate program as an adjunct. You likely need a terminal degree to teach in any graduate program; and some particular graduate programs, such as Law, require that you have worked in that degree field for a number of years before you can teach it.

Faculty Recruitment

Most schools will have a neat little packet to read or a contact person that you can speak with about faculty recruitment. Those that make finding the human resources department or applying difficult should be looked on with some skepticism. There is no reason to keep faculty recruitment practices a secret, unless they have something to hide.

Professional Responsibility

I firmly believe that we faculty who participate in this industry have a responsibility to help vet and professionally critique the schools we come across. I have a blog set up on my website for this very reason. I hope you will notify me if you run across any unethical educational practices. I wouldn't want to include schools with those methods in this publication.

University Human Resources

Where possible, I provided you direct links to the HR site for each of these schools. I also provided as much other contact information as was available to me at this writing.

Online Schools & Programs

American InterContinental University Online
careers.aiuonline.edu/careers/

Anthem College
www.anthemcollege.com/

Art Institute Online
www.aionline.edu/aboutus/online_learning_careers.asp

Ashford University
400 North Bluff Blvd
Clinton, IA 52732
www.ashford.edu/jobs/

Axia College Online
www.axiacollege.com/Faculty/index.asp

Capella University
www.capella.edu/careers/capella_careers_index.aspx

Cardean
111 N. Canal Street, Suite 455
Chicago, IL 60606
Phone: 1.866.948.1289.
(1.312.669.5289 if outside the U.S.)
http://cardean.edu/

Colorado Technical University Online
4435 North Chestnut Street · Suite E ·
Colorado Springs, CO 80907 ·
1-800-416-8904
www.ctuonline.edu

ECPI Online College of Technology
secure.recruitingcenter.net/Clients/school/PublicJobs/Canviewjobs.cfm?

Ellis College
ellis.nyit.edu/

Everest
everestinstitute.official-edu.com

FMU Online
www.fmuonline.com/contactus.php?schoolLocation=FMU%20Online

Kaplan University
www.kaplan.edu/careers/default.aspx

Minnesota School of Business
www.msbcollege.edu/about_us/msbjobs/

Saint Leo University
Human Resources MC2327
P. O. Box 6665
Saint Leo, FL 33574
Fax: 352-588-8249
www.saintleo.edu/SaintLeo/Templates/
Inner.aspx?pid=3123&proxy.pid=363

Stonecliffe
Stonecliffe.Online-College.org

Strayer University
www.strayer.edu

University of Phoenix Online

Phone: 800-546-7236
E-Mail: onlineaa@email.phoenix.edu
www.uopxonline.com/ContactInfo

University Alliance Schools
Saint Leo University
Regis University
University of Scranton
Florida Intitute of Technology
Jacksonville University
Tulane University
University of Notre Dame
Thunderbird
Villanova University

University of South Florida
http://www.universityalliance.com/info/

Villanova University
(610) 519-4235
Fax: (610) 519-6667
www.hr.villanova.edu

Westwood College Online
www2.westwoodonline.edu/information/
default.asp?NavPageID=38655

Criminal Justice
Edu. Paraprofessional/Teacher's Aide
Online Schools & Programs
General Studies
Java
Law Enforcement
Management
Medical Assisting
Medical Office Management
Medical Transcription
Networking
Paralegal Studies
Private Security
Programming
Web Development
Wireless Networking

Axia College Online
Accounting
Business
Criminal Justice
General Studies
Health Administration
Information Technology
Visual Communication
American InterContinental University Online
Business Administration Criminal Justice Healthcare Administration
Human Resources
Visual Communication

Associates Programs

Kaplan University Online
Accounting
Computer Information Systems
Corrections

Saint Leo University
Business Administration
Liberal Arts
University of Phoenix Online
General Studies
Information Technology/Net-

working
Paraprofessional Education

Westwood College Online
Computer Network Engineering
Graphic Design & Multimedia
Software Engineering

Ellis College
Accounting
Communication Arts
Finance
Management
Marketing
Telecommunications Technology

ECPI Online College of Technology
Accounting Administration
Business Systems Administration
Computer Electronics Engineering
Criminal Justice
IT/Networking & Security Mgmt

FMU Online
Accounting
Business Admin
Computer Info. Science
Criminal Investigations
Criminal Justice
Homeland Security
Paralegal

Strayer University
Accounting
Acquisition & Contract Mgmt
Business Management
Computer Info Systems
Computer Networking
Database Technology
Economics

General Studies
Internetworking Technology
Marketing

Anthem College
Business Management
Criminal Justice
Graphic Design
Health Management
Medical Billing & Coding
Technology Management

Everest
Accounting
Business
Criminal Investigations
Criminal Justice

Art Institute Online
Graphic Design
Interactive Media Design

Stonecliffe
Accounting
Business Administration
Criminal Justice
Medical Billing and Coding
Minnesota School of Business
Accounting & Tax Specialist
Business Administration
Cosmetology Business
Management Accounting
Paralegal
Transportation Business
Online Schools & Programs

Ashford University
Business
Bachelor Programs

Kaplan University Online
Accounting

Advanced Start in Communications
Advanced Start in Legal Studies
Alternative Dispute Resolution
Business (Advanced Start Bachelor's)
Business
Business Security and Assurance
Communications
Corrections
Crime Analysis
Crime Scene Investigation
Criminal Justice (Advanced Start Bachelor's)
Criminal Justice
E-Business
Finance
Forensic Psychology
Fraud Examination
Human Resource Management
Information Technology
IT (Advanced Start Bachelor's)
IT - Database
IT - Multimedia and Animation
IT - Networking
Law Enforcement
Legal Studies
Management (Advanced Start Bachelor's)
Management
Management of Info Systems
Nursing
Office Management
Organizational Communication
Paralegal (Advanced Start Bachelor's)
Paralegal Studies
Personal Injury
Private Security
Sales and Marketing
Technical Writing

University of Phoenix Online
Accounting
Business Administration
Business Communication
Business Management
Business/Public Administration
Communications
Criminal Justice
E-Business
Finance
Global Business
Health Admin/Health Info. Systems
Health Administration
Health Information Systems
Hospitality Management
Human Services & Mgmt
Information Systems
Information Systems Security
Information Technology
Long Term Care
Management
Marketing
Organizational Security
Psychology
Retail Management
RN to Bachelor of Science in Nursing
Supply Chain and Operations
Visual Communications

American InterContinental University Online
Accounting & Finance
Business Administration
Computer Forensics
Computer Systems
Criminal Justice
Healthcare Management
Human Resources
Information Technology
International Business

Internet Security
Marketing
Network Administration
Operations Management
Organizational Psychology
Programming
Project Management
Visual Communication
Web Design – Bachelor's Degree

Kennedy Western University
Computer Science
E-Business/E-Commerce
Electrical Engineering
Environmental Engineering
Finance
General Engineering
Management & Leadership
Management of Technology
Mechanical Engineering
Quality Control (Bachelor's / Master's)
Safety Engineering
Software Engineering
Online Schools & Programs

Ellis College
Accounting/Professional Accounting
Advertising
Criminal Justice
Distributed Database Systems
Electronics and Information Security
English/Literature & Culture
English/Professional Writing
Finance
General Management
Hospitality Management
Human Resources Management
Information and Network Security
Interactive Multimedia

Interd. Studies/Behavioral Sciences
Interd. Studies/Business
Interd. Studies/Communication Arts
Interd. Studies/Computer Science
Interd. Studies/English
Interd. Studies/Hospitality Mgmt
Interd. Studies/Humanities
Interd. Studies/Labor Relations
Interd. Studies/Math/Physics
Interd. Studies/Social Sciences
Interd. Studies/Technical Writing
Interd. Studies/Technology
Interd. Studies/Telecommunications Mgmt
International Business
Internet Engineering
Management of Information Systems
Managerial Accounting
Marketing
Political Science
Psychology
Small Business & Entrepreneurship
Sociology
Telecommunications Network Mgmt

Colorado Technical University Online
Accounting
Criminal Justice
Finance
Health Care Management
Human Resources
Information Technology
Management
Marketing
Project Management
Software Eng./Network Mgmt

Software Engineering
Software Engineering/Security
Capella University
Accounting
Business Administration
Finance
Graphics & Multimedia
Human Resource Management
Information Assurance and Security
Information Technology
Management and Leadership
Marketing
Network Technology
Project Management
Web Application Development

Saint Leo University
Accounting
Business / Health Care Management
Business Admin / Accounting
Business Management
Computer Information Systems
Criminal Justice

Westwood College Online
Accounting
Animation
Business/Marketing & Sales
Computer Network Management
Criminal justice
E-Business Management
Fashion Merchandising
Game Art and Design
Game Software Development
Information Systems Security
Interior Design
Visual Communications
Web Design & Multimedia

FMU Online
Accounting
Business Admin
Computer Info. Science
Criminal Justice
Homeland Security
Paralegal

Ashford University
Org Mgmt/Accounting
Org Mgmt/Advertising
Org Mgmt/Biology
Org Mgmt/Business
Org Mgmt/Business Administration
Org Mgmt/Child Study
Org Mgmt/Communications
Org Mgmt/Computer Graphic Design
Org Mgmt/Criminal Justice
Org Mgmt/Early Childhood Education
Org Mgmt/Education
Org Mgmt/Elementary Education
Org Mgmt/Engineering Studies
Org Mgmt/English/Language Arts
Org Mgmt/Fashion Merchandising
Org Mgmt/Finance
Org Mgmt/Health Care Administration
Org Mgmt/History
Org Mgmt/Hospitality Management
Org Mgmt/Human Resources
Org Mgmt/Human Services Administration
Org Mgmt/Human Services Administration
Org Mgmt/Liberal Studies
Org Mgmt/Management
Org Mgmt/Mathematics

Org Mgmt/Physical Education
Org Mgmt/Political Science
Org Mgmt/Psychology
Org Mgmt/Public Administration
Org Mgmt/Sociology
Psychology

Strayer University
Accounting Business Management
Computer Info Systems
Computer Networking
Database Technology
Economics
Human Resource Management
International Business Internetworking
Technology Legal Studies
Marketing

Argosy University
Bachelor of Arts (BA) in Psychology (Degree Completion Program)
Bachelor of Science (BS) in Business Administration

Anthem College
Business Management Criminal Justice
Health Management Technology Management

Western Governors University
B.A. in Mathematics (5-9 or 9-12)
B.A. in Science (5-9 or 9-12)
B.A. in Social Science (5-12)
B.S. in Accounting
B.S. in IT- Networks Administration Emphasis
B.S. in IT- Networks Design and

Management
B.S. Information Technology
B.S. Information Technology-Databases
Emphasis
B.S. Information Technology-Security Emphasis
B.S. Information Technology-Software Emphasis Business
Management Business/IT Mgmt
Finance Human Resource Management
Marketing Management

Art Institute Online
Advertising Game Art and Design
Graphic Design Interactive Media
Design Interior Design Media
Arts and Animation

Everest
Criminal Justice
Minnesota School of Business
Accounting Business Administration Paralegal

Jones International University
Accounting Communication
Management
General Busiess Sales and Marketing Sales and Marketing Mgmt

Walden University Online
Business Administration Finance
Human
Resource Management Information
Systems Management Marketing

Grand Canyon University
Elementary Education/English
Elementary Education/Math

Elementary Education/Science
Healthcare Management
Nursing (RN to Bachelor's)
South University
Business Administration
Criminal Justice / Crime Scene
Criminal Justice / Cyber Crime
Criminal Justice / Juvenile Justice
Criminal Justice / Law Enforce.
Criminal Justice /Corrections
Finance
Healthcare Management
Info Technology / Database
Admin
Info Technology / Network
Admin
Info Technology / Web Mgmt
Information Technology
Management and Leadership
Marketing
Nursing (RN to BSN)

Certificate Programs

ECPI Online College of Technology
Networking & Security Management - Bachelor's

Kaplan University Online
Case Management
Computer Programming Language
Executive Coaching
Financial Planning
Forensic Nursing
Geriatric Care Management
Information Technology Pathway
Internet and Web Development

Iowa Teacher Intern
Legal Nurse Consulting
Life Care Planning
Master of Education (Iowa)
Postbaccalaureate Pathway to
Paralegal
Professional Development for
Teachers
Project Management
Risk Management

Villanova University
Contract Management
Information Systems Security
Phillips ROI Methodology
Project Management
Project Management-IS/IT
Six Sigma
Software Testing

Strayer University
Accounting
Accounting (Undergrad Cert.)
Accounting Info Systems
Acquisition & Contract Mgmt
Business Management
Business Management
Computer Info Systems
Computer Info Systems
Computer Information Systems
Internetworking Technology
Network Security
Web Development

University of Phoenix Online
Call Center Professional
Human Resource Management
Integrative Health Care
Nursing Health Care Education
Project Management

Cardean

Business Administration
Computers in Education
Corporate Governance
Distance Learning
Finance
Human Resources Management
International Business
Leadership
Management of Information
Systems
Marketing
Multimedia Dev. for Educ. and
Training
Professional Accounting
Strategy and Economics

University of Notre Dame
Advanced Negotiations
Executive Negotiation
Negotiation Essentials
Strategies for Conflict Mgmt
Thunderbird
International Marketing (Executive)
International Mgmt (Executive)

Art Institute Online
Web Design

Tulane University
Advanced Management Strategy
Advanced Marketing Strategy
Business Essentials I
Business Essentials II
Master Cert. Business Management
Master Cert. Business Marketing

Ellis College
Accounting
Distance Learning
Finance

International Business
Management of Information
Systems
Marketing
Multimedia
Technical Writing

Minnesota School of Business
Accounting
Business Admin Assistant
Project Management

Doctoral Program

Walden University Online
Admin. Leadership for Teaching
& Learning (Ed.D)
Applied Mgmt & Decision Sciences (Ph.D.)
Doctor of Education (Ed.D.)
Education (Ph.D.)
Health Services (Ph.D)
Human Services (Ph.D)
Psychology (Ph.D.)
Public Health (Ph.D.)
Public Policy & Administration
(Ph.D.)
Capella University
Counseling Studies
Criminal Justice
Curriculum and Instruction
Educational Psychology
General Human Services
General Psychology
Health Care Administration
Human Resource Management
Industrial/Organiz. Psychology
Information Tech Management
Instructional Design
K-12 Studies in Education

Leadership
Leadership for Higher Education
Leadership in Educational Administration
Management Non-Profit Agencies
Organization & Management
Postsecondary & Adult Education
Professional Studies in Education
Social Work & Community Serv.
Training and Performance Improvement

University of Phoenix Online
Business Administration
Educational Leadership
Health Administration
Information Systems
Organizational Leadership

Kennedy Western University
Computer Science
Engineering Management
Environmental Engineering
General Engineering
International Business Administration
Management Info Systems
Safety Engineering

Argosy University
Business Administration
Clinical Psychology (PsyD)
Community College Executive
Leadership
Counseling Psychology
Counselor Education and Supervision
Edu. Specialist in School Counseling
Educational Leadership
Educational Specialist in Ed
Leadership

Educational Specialist in Instructional Leadership
Instructional Leadership
Organizational Leadership
Pastoral Community Counseling
School Psychology (PsyD)

Concord Law School
Executive JD (Law Degree)
Juris Doctor (Law Degree)

Master's Degree Programs

Ellis College
Accounting and Information
Systems
Business Administration
E-Commerce
Finance
Global Management
Health Care Administration
Human Resources Management
Leadership
Management of Info. Systems
Management of Technology
Marketing
Professional Accounting
Project Management
Risk Management
Strategy and Economics

Kaplan University Online
Entrepreneurship
Finance
Human Resource Management
Information Technology
Management, Comm, and Quality
Marketing
Master's - Business Administra-

tion

University of Phoenix Online
Accounting
Global Management
Health Care Management
Human Resources
Marketing
Master of Business Administra-
tion
MSN/MBA/HCM
Public Administration
Technology Management

Capella University
Accounting
Business Administration
Finance
Health Care Management
Information Tech Management
Marketing
Project Management

**American InterContinental
University Online**
Accounting & Finance
Business Administration
Healthcare Management
Human Resources
International Business
Marketing
Operations Management
Organizational Psychology -
Project Management

Cardean
Accounting and Information
Systems
Business Administration
E-Commerce
Finance

Financial Analysis
Financial Planning
Health Care Administration
Hospitality Management
Human Resources Management
International Business
Leadership
Management of Information
Systems
Management of Technology
Marketing
MBA Fast Track
Operations/Supply Chain Man-
agement
Professional Accounting
Project Management
Risk Management
Small Business/Entrepreneurship
Strategy and Economics
Regis University
MBA / Business Admin
MBA / Finance & Accounting
MBA / Health Care Mgmt
MBA / Marketing

South University
Healthcare Administration
Master of Business Administra-
tion

**Saint Leo University Masters
Programs**
Accounting
Criminal Justice
General Business
Human Resource Administration

**Colorado Technical University
Online**
Accounting
Executive Master of Business
Administration

Finance
Health Care Management
Human Resource Management
Info Technology Management
Management
Project Management

FMU Online
Master of Business Administration
Strayer University
Business Management

Western Governors University
Master of Business Administration
MBA/IT Management

Minnesota School of Business
Masters in Business Administration

Jones International University
Accounting
Entrepreneurship
Finance
Global Enterprise Management
Health Care Management
Info Technology Management
Information Security Management
Negotiation & Conflict Mgmt
Project Management

Walden University Online
Business Administration
Business Process Management
eBusiness
Emerging Technologies
Engineering Innovation
Finance
Global Business

Global Product Management
Health Services
Human Resources Management
Information Strategies
Knowledge Management
Management of Technology
Marketing
Nonprofit Management
Risk Management/Insurance
Technology Project Management

Grand Canyon University
Executive MBA
Health Systems Management
Nursing Leadership (MBA/Master's)

Argosy University
Master of Business Administration

Tiffin University
Master of Business Administration

Walden University Online
Computer Engineering
Computer Science
Education
Electrical Engineering
Elementary Reading & Literacy
Elementary Reading and Mathematics
Engineering Management
M.S. in Nursing (BSN - MSN)/ Education
M.S. in Nursing (BSN - MSN)/ Leadership & Mgmt
M.S. in Nursing (BSN – MSN)
M.S. in Nursing (RN - MSN)
M.S. in Nursing (RN - MSN)/ Education

M.S. in Nursing (RN - MSN)/
Leadership & Mgmt
Master of Public Administration
Master of Public Health
Mental Health Counseling
Psychology
Software Engineering
Systems Engineering

Kaplan University Online
Corrections
Criminal Justice
Education - Teaching and Learn-
ing
Entrepreneurship
Finance
Global Issues
Human Resource Management
Information Technology
Law
Leadership and Executive Mgmt
Management, Comm, and Quality
Marketing
Master's - Business Administra-
tion
Policing
Teaching Literacy & Language
6-12
Teaching Literacy & Language
K-6
Teaching Mathematics 6-8
Teaching Mathematics 9-12
Teaching Mathematics K-5
Teaching Science 6-12
Teaching Science K-6
Teaching Students w/Special
Needs
Teaching w/Technology

Capella University
Business Administration
Clinical Psychology

Counseling Psychology
Counseling Studies
Criminal Justice
Curriculum and Instruction
Educational Psychology
Finance
General Human Services Program
General Psychology
Health Care Administration
Health Care Management
Human Resource Management
Industrial/Organiz. Psychology
Information Security
Information Technology
Information Tech Management
Information Tech Management
Instructional Design Online
Learning
K-12 Studies in Education
Leadership
Leadership for Higher Education
Leadership in Educational Admin-
istration
Management Non-Profit Agencies
Marital/Couple/Family Counsel-
ing
Marketing
Mental Health Counseling
Network Architecture and Design
Organization & Management
Postsecondary & Adult Education
Professional Studies in Education
Project Management
Project Management
School Psychology
Social Work & Community Serv.
Sport Psychology
System Design and Programming
Training and Performance Im-
provement

University of Phoenix Online

Accounting
Administration and Supervision
Computer Info Systems
Curriculum & Instruction-Adult Ed.
Curriculum & Instruction-Computer Ed.
Curriculum & Instruction-ESL Ed.
Curriculum and Instruction
Online Schools & Programs
Early Childhood Education
Elementary Teacher Education
Global Management
Health Administration
Health Care Management
Healthcare/Nursing
Human Resource Mgmt
Human Resources
IS/Management
Justice and Security
Management
Marketing
Master of Business Administration
Master of Science in Nursing
Master's in Nursing (Health Care Education)
Master's in Nursing (Integrative Health Care)
MSN/MBA/HCM
Nursing and Health Admin
Organizational Management
Public Administration
Public Administration
Secondary Teacher Education
Special Education
Technology Management

American InterContinental University Online
Accounting & Finance

Business Administration
Education
Education-Conc. Curriculum & Instruc.
Education-Conc. Ed. Assess. & Eval.
Education-Conc. Instructional Tech.
Education-Conc. Leader in Ed. Org.
Healthcare Management
Human Resources
Information Technology
International Business
Marketing
Operations Management
Organizational Psychology -
Project Management
South University
Criminal Justice
Healthcare Administration
Master of Business Administration
Nursing

Ellis College
Accounting & Information Systems
Advertising and Public Relations
Business Administration
Computer Science
E-Commerce
Finance
Global Management
Health Care Administration
Human Resources Management
Human Resources Mgmt & Labor Relations
Instructional Technology Educators
Instructional Technology for Trainers

Leadership
Management of Info. Systems
Management of Technology
Marketing
Professional Accounting
Project Management
Risk Management
Strategy and Economics
FMU Online
Criminal Justice

Kennedy Western University
Computer Science
Engineering Management
Environmental Engineering
Executive Business Administration
General Engineering
Human Resource Management
Management Info Systems
Management of Technology
Quality Control
Safety Engineering

Cardean
Accounting & Information Systems
Business Administration
Communication Arts/Advertising/PR
Communication Arts/Journalism
E-Commerce
Finance
Financial Analysis
Financial Planning
Health Care Administration
Hospitality Management
Human Resources Management
Information Management
Instructional Technology for

Educators
Instructional Technology for
Professional
Trainers
International Business
Leadership
Management of Information
Systems
Management of Technology
Marketing
MBA Fast Track
Operations/Supply Chain Management
Professional Accounting
Project Management
Risk Management
Small Business/Entrepreneurship
Strategy and Economics

Colorado Technical University Online
Accounting
Executive Master of Business
Administration
Finance
Health Care Management
Human Resource Management
Info Technology Management
Information Systems Security
Management
Project Management

Saint Leo University Masters Programs
Accounting
Criminal Justice
General Business
Human Resource Administration

Strayer University
Accounting Info Systems
Business Management

Communications Technology
Educational Management
Health Services Admin
Information Systems
Information Systems Mgmt.
Public Administration
Technology in Education

Regis University
MBA / Business Admin
MBA / Finance & Accounting
MBA / Health Care Mgmt
MBA / Marketing

University of Scranton
Education - Curriculum & Instruction
Education - Educational Administration
Florida Tech University Online
Systems Management/Info Systems
Western Governors University
Learning and Technology
Math Ed. (K-6, 5-9, or 5-12)

Science Ed. (5-9 or 5-12)
Teaching (PK-8)
Teaching-Math (5-9 or 9-12)
Teaching-Science (5-9 or 9-12)
Teaching-Social Science (5-12)
Management and Innovation
Master of Business Administration
MBA/IT Management
Measurement & Evaluation

Grand Canyon University
Curriculum & Instruction
Curriculum & Instruction/Tech
Education Administration
Education Admn / Org. Leadership
Educational Admin / School
Leadership
Elementary Ed(elgible for IRC)
Elementary Education
Executive MBA
Health Systems Management
Nursing Leadership (MBA/Master's)
Nursing Leadership in Healthcare
Secondary Ed (eligible for IRC)
Secondary Education
Special Ed for Certified Special
Educators
Special Education (eligible for
IRC)
Special Education
Teaching
Teaching English (TESOL)
Minnesota School of Business
Masters in Business Administration

Jones International University
Accounting
Adult Education & Administration
Corporate Training & Knowledge
Mgmt
Educational Leadership & Administration
Elementary Curriculum, Instruction & Assessment
Entrepreneurship
Finance
Global Enterprise Management
Health Care Management
Info Technology Management
Information Security Management

Leadership and Influence
Leading the Customer-Driven
Org.
Negotiation & Conflict Mgmt
Project Management
Secondary Curriculum, Instruc-
tion & Assessment
Technology and Design

Argosy University
Clinical Psych./Marriage & Fam-
ily Therapy
Clinical Psychology
Counseling Psychology
Counseling Psychology/Marriage
& Family Therapy
Educational Leadership
Forensic Psychology
Guidance Counseling
Instructional Leadership
Marriage and Family Therapy
Mental Health Counseling
Professional Counseling
School Psychology
Sport-Exercise Psychology
Tiffin University
Master of Arts in Humanities
Master of Business Administra-
tion
Master of Science: Crime Analy-
sis
Master of Science: Homeland
Security Admin
Master of Science: Justice Admin.

Ashford University
Arts in Teaching & Learning
Business Administration
Communications Technology
Educational Management
Health Services Admin
Information Systems

Information Systems Mgmt.
Public Administration
Technology in Education
Regis University
MBA / Business Admin
MBA / Finance & Accounting
MBA / Health Care Mgmt
MBA / Marketing

University of Scranton
Education - Curriculum & Instruction
Education - Educational Administration

Florida Tech University Online
Systems Management/Info Systems

Western Governors University
Learning and Technology
Math Ed. (K-6, 5-9, or 5-12)
Science Ed. (5-9 or 5-12)
Teaching (PK-8)
Teaching-Math (5-9 or 9-12)
Teaching-Science (5-9 or 9-12)
Teaching-Social Science (5-12)
Management and Innovation
Master of Business Administra-
tion
MBA/IT Management
Measurement & Evaluation

Grand Canyon University
Curriculum & Instruction
Curriculum & Instruction/Tech
Education Administration
Education Admn / Org. Leader-
ship
Educational Admin / School
Leadership
Elementary Ed(elgible for IRC)

Elementary Education
Executive MBA
Health Systems Management
Nursing Leadership (MBA/Master's)
Nursing Leadership in Healthcare
Secondary Ed (eligible for IRC)
Secondary Education
Special Ed for Certified Special Educators
Special Education (eligible for IRC)
Special Education
Teaching
Teaching English (TESOL)

Minnesota School of Business
Masters in Business Administration

Jones International University
Accounting
Adult Education & Administration
Corporate Training & Knowledge Mgmt
Educational Leadership & Administration
Elementary Curriculum, Instruction & Assessment
Entrepreneurship
Finance
Global Enterprise Management
Health Care Management
Info Technology Management
Information Security Management
Leadership and Influence
Leading the Customer-Driven Org.
Negotiation & Conflict Mgmt
Project Management

Secondary Curriculum, Instruction & Assessment
Technology and Design

Argosy University
Clinical Psych./Marriage & Family Therapy
Clinical Psychology
Counseling Psychology
Counseling Psychology/Marriage & Family Therapy
Educational Leadership
Forensic Psychology
Guidance Counseling
Instructional Leadership
Marriage and Family Therapy
Mental Health Counseling
Professional Counseling
School Psychology
Sport-Exercise Psychology

Tiffin University
Master of Arts in Humanities
Master of Business Administration
Master of Science: Crime Analysis
Master of Science: Homeland Security Admin
Master of Science: Justice Admin.

Ashford University
Arts in Teaching & Learning
Business Administration

About The Author

Rebecca Brown has taught more than 3000 courses online. She teaches at between five and 10 schools at any given time. She also trains online faculty and serves as a mentor for new adjuncts.

She is the author of several Short & Sweet titles, including *How to Study Smart Not Hard*, and *How to Make As in eCollege*, which can be found at www.ShortandSweetBooks.com.

Becky divides her time between her home in New York City and the family cabin on the Puget Sound. She loves to talk to other full-time adjuncts about their online teaching and is always happy to answer questions, help with problems, and applaud successes in the eCollege world.

You may email Becky at:
BeckyBrown@ShortandSweetBooks.com

Made in the USA
Lexington, KY
26 September 2012